when i
fall

poems

Sabina Laura

CASTLE POINT BOOKS
NEW YORK

WHEN I FALL. Copyright © 2024 by St. Martin's Press. All rights reserved.

Printed in the United States of America. For information,
address St. Martin's Publishing Group, 120 Broadway, New York, NY 10271.

www.castlepointbooks.com

The Castle Point Books trademark is owned by Castle Point Publishing, LLC.
Castle Point books are published and distributed by St. Martin's Publishing Group.

ISBN 978-1-250-28801-1 (trade paperback)
ISBN 978-1-250-28817-2 (ebook)

Design by Melissa Gerber
Edited by Monica Sweeney

Images used under license by Shutterstock.com.

Our books may be purchased in bulk for promotional, educational, or business use.

Please contact your local bookseller or the Macmillan Corporate and
Premium Sales Department at 1-800-221-7945, extension 5442, or by email
at MacmillanSpecialMarkets@macmillan.com.

First Edition: 2024

10 9 8 7 6 5 4 3 2 1

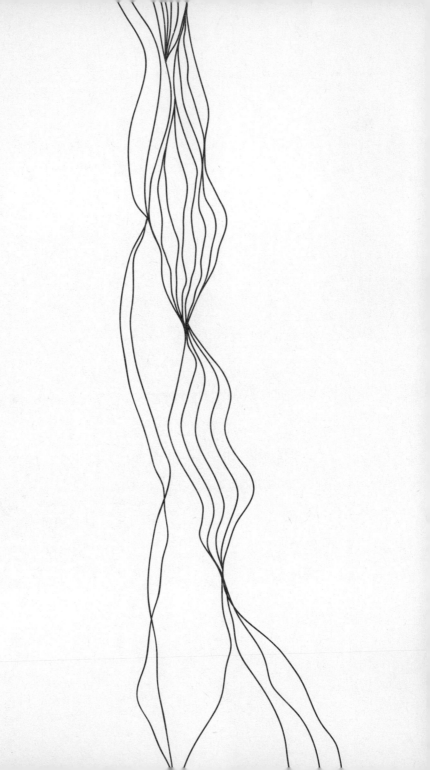

Falling

When I Fall

When I fall,
you are a soft landing,
like raindrops
on branches,
like autumn leaves
to the forest floor.
But it is so easy
to fall for you
without caring
where I might land.

Walls

It won't be easy
to break down my walls.
I've built them so high
and so sturdy
that the only way
is to climb over them.
But I won't apologize
for the ways I've
protected this heart.
It's the reason
I still have so much
love to give.

Between Fear and Falling

There is a moment
in the space between fear and falling
where something beautiful happens.

Like a line in the sand,
a point of no return,

Where the tide comes in
and washes all the worry away.

Where love is a new horizon
and all I want to do is reach for it.

Where you are an ocean
that needs to be discovered
and suddenly drowning is not a word I know.

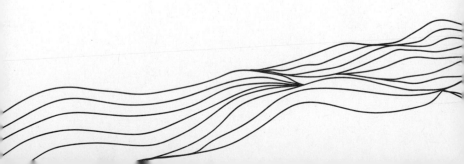

Over the Edge

I'm peering over the edge
with brave eyes, but my hands
are still holding on.

My mind mutters,
What if it breaks me?

While my heart whispers,
But what if it makes me?

The Perfect Balance

Let your heart stay tender—
to love in the same way as ever
But let it be tough enough to know
when you deserve better.

To Trust Someone
with Your Heart

To trust someone
with your heart
is to let them see
the fragile, messy way
it's held together
and hope they won't
pull at the stitches
or pick at the glue.

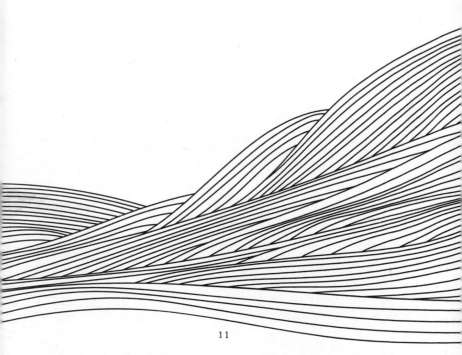

The Moment We Met

You looked at me
like I was a sunset
you'd always remember.

I was already hoping
you'd still be there
by dawn.

A Mess of Everything

Let's make a mess
of everything.

Let's keep our hearts
beautifully open
and fall wildly
into love.

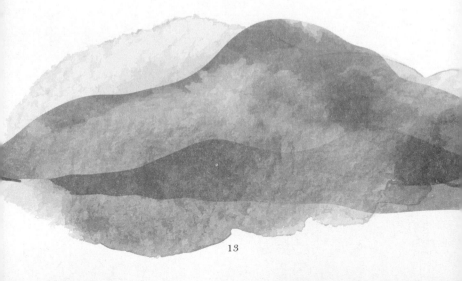

The Fall

This time,
I will let myself fall.

Because even if
you're not there
to catch me,
I know I've still got my wings.

Believe

I like to believe that the people who were
meant to find us will.
The hands that were meant to hold us
won't let go.
The eyes that were meant to see us will
never look away.
The hearts that were meant to love us
always will.
And the ones who don't belong will be the
only ones who choose to leave.

I like to believe that the universe has a plan.
That fate is real and there's a reason why
life happens the way it does.
And in the end, we will all find the people
meant for us.

My Heart Is a House

My heart is a house
and I'm fussy about who I let in.

If I open the door for you,
I'll ask you to wipe your feet
and be careful not to break anything
(because it's all far more fragile
than you'd expect).

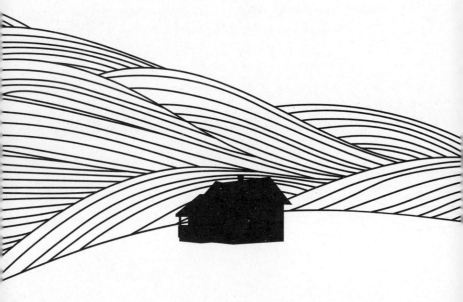

And you can make yourself at home
as long as you promise
not to overstay your welcome
(because there isn't room in the attic
for any more ghosts).

But if you treat it with care,
maybe I'll invite you to stay.
Maybe I'll even get a key cut for you.

Jump

I am learning
to love
without fear.
So I take
a deep breath
and I jump
into the unknown,
trusting
that your hands
will catch me.

The Countdown

You'll have to be patient with me.
I don't know how to love
without expecting the worst.

It always seems
to be a waiting game,
just a countdown until
it turns into another loss.

(But I hope you'll be the one
to prove me wrong.)

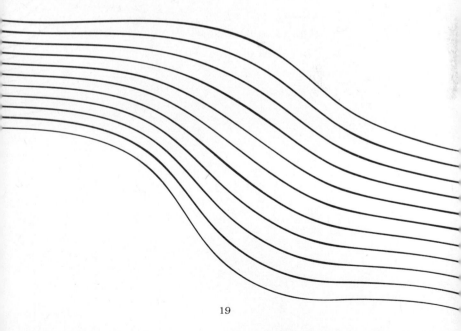

Opening

I will become
a window.
A locket.
A budding flower.
A key inside of a lock.
A butterfly unfurling its wings.

I will keep looking
for new ways to open
my heart to you.

If It's Meant to Stay

The hard part
is that loss
is the risk you must take
for love.

The easy part
is knowing that
if it's meant to stay,
it will.

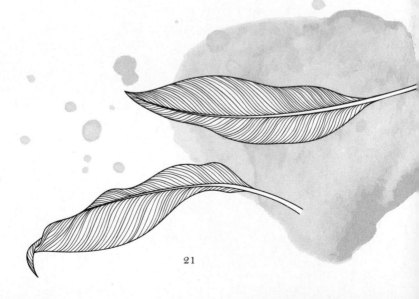

No Turning Back

It's all too easy to stay right where I am,
a comfortable distance between us.
It can't go wrong from here.
My heart is safe,
but it isn't satisfied.

I am too curious—
I want to find out what we might become.
Courage tells me
to take a step closer to you
and longing pulls me forward.

My heart is hurtling toward yours
at a million miles per hour
and I know there's no turning back.
But I wouldn't stop regardless.

If I crash violently
into your rejection,
I know that loving you would be
the most beautiful way
my heart could break.

Native Tongue

I do not speak in
half love
or uncertain love.

It has to be forever love.
It's the only language I know.

Tangled

My heart is tangled up in you
and all the little things you do,
and I don't ever want it to unravel.

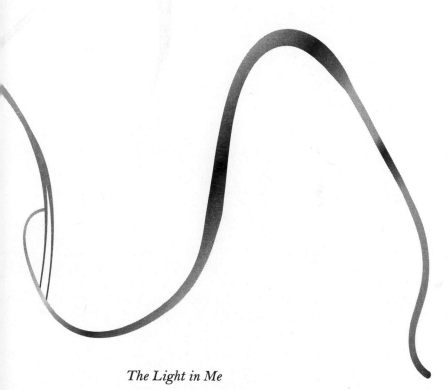

The Light in Me

You met me at dusk,
and I showed you
all the ways the dark gets in.

But you painted me in sunshine
until even I could see
the light in me.

Ready to Surrender

If you are wondering
when I will be willing
to let love in again,
know that fear does not
live here anymore.
My arms are as open as my heart
and they are both waiting
to welcome you.

Once and Forever

You are a once-in-a-lifetime kind of love,
and I don't ever want to lose you—
It would always be too soon.

You Saw Me

You still saw me
even when I tried
to be invisible,

and I forgot
all the reasons
I wanted to hide.

Tumbling

There was something about him
that caused a fault in my system.
By the time my head warned me
how dangerous the drop could be,
my heart was already tumbling.

Eternity

Remove your mask
and reveal the glorious
mess within.

I want to spend an eternity learning you.
I want to spend an eternity loving you.

Fate

I think it was fate—

The way the radio station
played my favorite song
just as I tuned in.

The way the rain stopped
as soon as I opened
my front door.

The way we fell together
just at the right moment—
when everything else was falling apart.

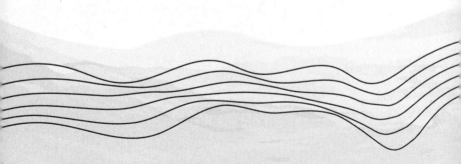

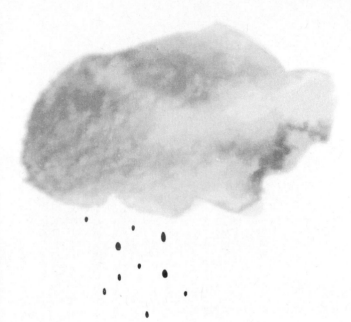

Made of Rain

Don't be scared
to show me
the parts of you
that are made of rain.

*I will love your storms
just as much as your light.*

My Heart Knows

My heart knows
what it wants.

A life full of
poetry and passion.
Meaning and magic.
Love and laughter.

That means
a life full of you.

Through Everything

I will love you
through everything—
the good days and bad ones,
every season and every storm,
because I know they all have
room for us to grow.

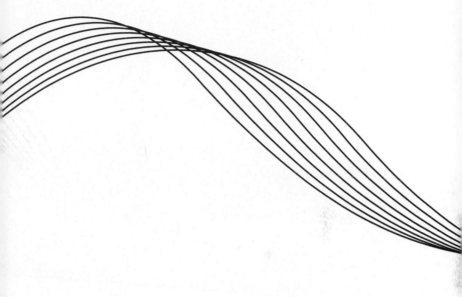

Where I Was Meant to Be

This love is a gravity
that cannot be fought against,
pulling two hearts together as one.
And when I gained enough courage
to let it guide me, I found
exactly where I was meant to be.

A Little Longer

We pressed fast forward on fear
to get to the good part
and then fell in slow motion
so we didn't miss a thing.
And if I could, I would replay
every single moment,
just to make forever
last a little longer.

You Were There

I was searching
for somewhere to land,
for something gentle
to break the fall,
and you were there,
ready to catch me,
as if all along,
you were waiting
for me to find
my way home.

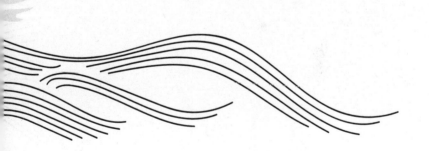

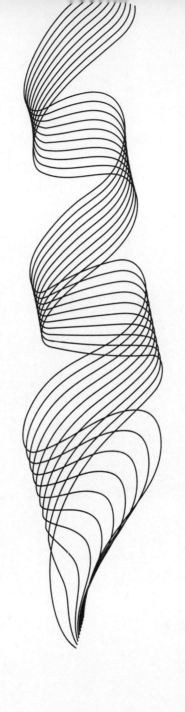

Spiraling

Lost Glow

You disappeared
like the sun
at dusk,

and I have been
searching for the light
ever since.

Loving You

Loving you was
a falling out of orbit.
A spiraling out of control.
A crash landing.
A shattering of the heart.

Even soft things can break
if there's no one there to catch them.

Won't You Stay

Won't you stay
just a while longer?

I am not ready to miss you.

Forest Fires

The spark between us
felt like magic
until there were forest fires
every way we turned,
and we knew that
the only way out of this
would leave us both
covered in burns.

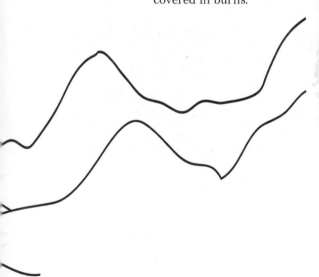

Butterflies

I used to think that
the way you made me feel
was how love should be.

Like the way you
took my breath away.
The way my heartbeat
only knew chaos
and not calm.

But now I know
that all along, the butterflies
were just trying to warn me:

It isn't safe to land here.

A Sad Story

We were just
a five-word sad story:

It wasn't meant to be.

The Last Leaf

I am the first
to anticipate a goodbye
but the last to accept it.

I see it coming for miles,
an autumn storm rolling in
across the hills.
But I am the last leaf
still clinging to the branches.

I know winter is coming
and I will have no choice
but to let go.
I still wait.

Just in case
the sun comes back.

The Break

I think I would take
each of my bones fracturing
a thousand times over
instead of my heart breaking
like this.

Nightfall

Nightfall is the loneliest time,
lying against tear-stained pillows instead of you.

But I haven't slept for weeks.

Instead, I talk to the moon about you
and she listens all night long,
and by dawn the circles under my eyes
have turned the color of *I miss you*.
But you have always been
my favorite shade of heartbreak.

Someday

You were my right place, right time,
but I was only ever your *someday,*

and it hurts to remember
how much I gave you
and how little I got back.

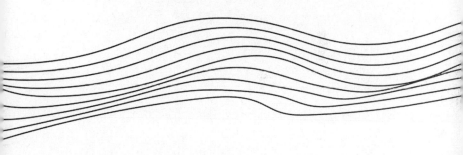

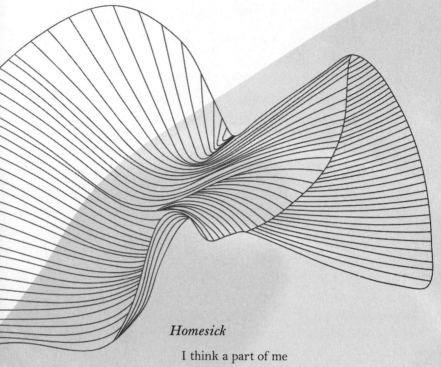

Homesick

I think a part of me
will always be homesick for us,
but when you stopped being a home
and became a haunted house,
I knew I couldn't stay.

Muscle Memory

I still check my phone for your name
and my driveway for your car,
and I still smell you on my pillowcases
no matter how many times they've been washed.
I still sleep on one half of the bed,
even though when I wake up
I roll toward your side
before I remember you're not there.
I still think I hear your key in the door
and you singing in the shower,
and I wonder how much time has to pass
before loving you stops being muscle memory.

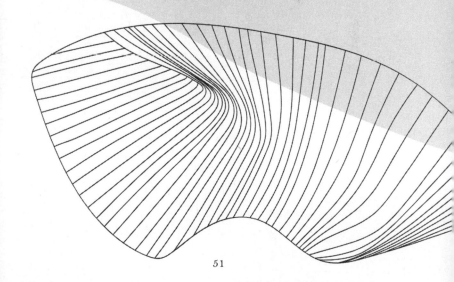

Abandon Ship

I keep pulling you closer, but still feel
an insurmountable distance between us,
like swirling oceans of loneliness.

It's time to abandon ship,
before it sinks us both.

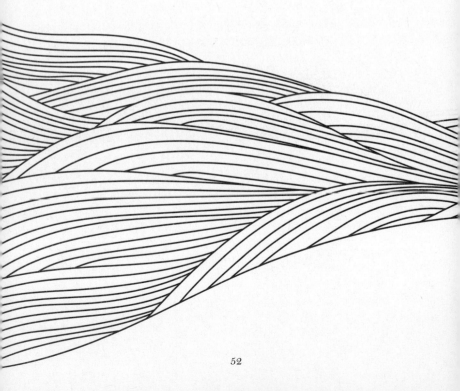

The Wreckage of Us

You seemed to escape unscathed
from the wreckage of us,
while I am still not sure
if there will ever be another day
I don't miss you.

You made forgetting look so easy,
and all I know how to do is remember.

The Phantom

Some nights
I cannot help
but let your ghost back in.

Don't you understand?
*Part of me wants
to be haunted forever.*

Battle Scars

Your love was a war
I never wanted to fight,

but you left me
covered in battle scars,

the kind that still hurt
long after they've stopped bleeding.

The Words Left Unsaid

The words left unsaid
echo 'round my mind
like raindrops splattering
the window.

But it's too late
to say them now.

You've already found blue skies.
You've already left our storm behind.

At the End

When you said
you wanted us to try again,
I knew it would be like
watching a movie we'd seen before
and hoping for a different ending.

But this time
you wouldn't be
my favorite character,
and I wouldn't stick around waiting
for the credits to roll,
knowing that there was
only more heartbreak
waiting for us
at the end.

One Day

You said *one day*
like you meant *soon*
because you knew I'd be there waiting.

You said *one day*
like you meant it as a promise,
but you never planned to keep it.

You just showed me a dream
that you would never make a reality
and left me somewhere up in the clouds.

You just planted a seed
of hope in my heart
and left it there to wilt.

Wishes

I will search the earth
for four-leaf clovers
and the sky for shooting stars.

I will break
a wishbone apart
and a fortune cookie open.

I will close my eyes
as I blow out candles
and throw pennies into fountains.

I will wait
for a clock to strike 11:11
and for a rainbow to appear.

And I know
I'm not supposed to tell,
but every wish will be for you.

The Hardest Part

Missing you hurts,
and there's so much
I could do about it.

I could call you to tell you,
but you wouldn't pick up.
I could send love letters,
but you wouldn't read them.
I could ask to meet you,
but you wouldn't show up.

And it wouldn't make any difference at all.
You still wouldn't miss me back.

In Seasons

This winter was so bitterly cold
that all the flowers died,
the fruit decayed before
we could enjoy its sweetness,
and distance became the only thing
that knew how to bloom.

We always loved in seasons
but there would never be
another spring.

Just Like You

I love harder
and stay longer,
and people tend to leave me
long before I could leave them.

Just like you.

I was still hoping
I was someone you never wanted to lose,
but you were already saying goodbye.

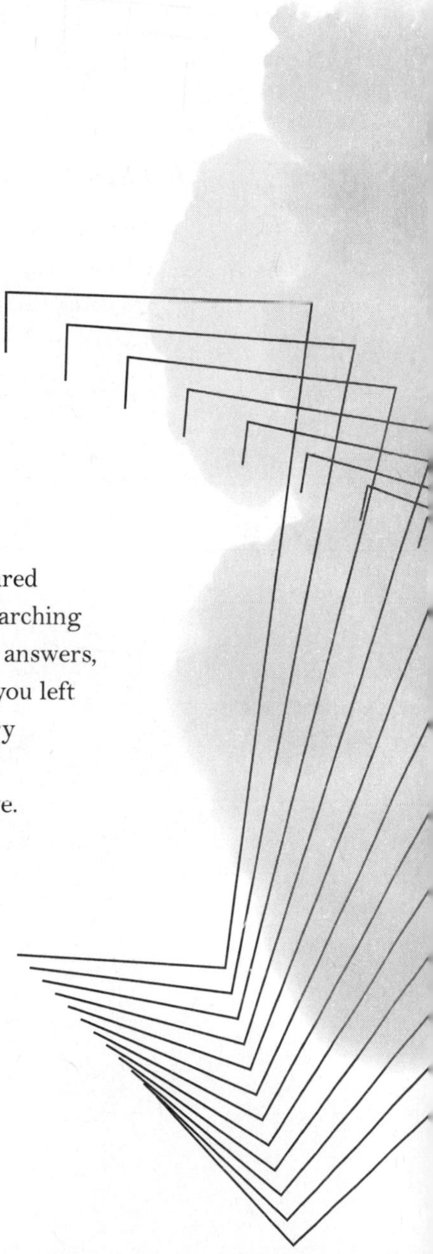

Mystery

You disappeared
and I kept searching
the abyss for answers,
but the way you left
was a mystery
I was never
going to solve.

Wound

A memory reopens the wound.

But I don't ever want to forget
the sound of your voice
when you said you loved me.

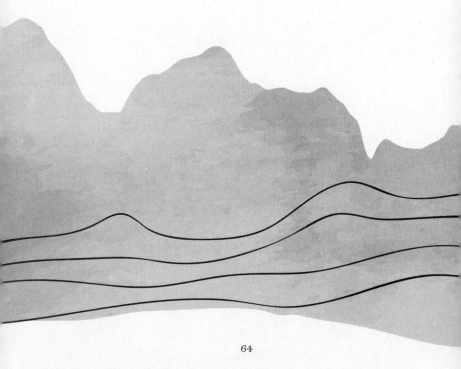

Chasing Echoes

I've been chasing echoes
from a love song
you no longer sing.
I'm not sure whether
you ever really meant the tune,
but I fear
this song will be stuck
in my head forever.

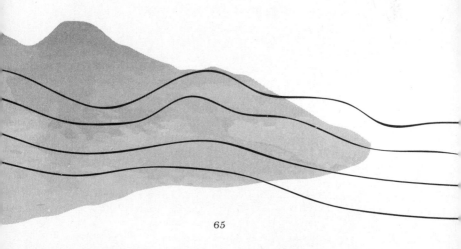

Avalanche

You left so quietly,
like falling snowflakes.

You thought
it would be gentler that way.

But to me it was an avalanche.

The Way I Ache for You

You linger in my thoughts
and echo in my memory,
and I don't always try to fight it.
Because the way I ache for you
is so beautiful that part of me
doesn't ever want to heal.

If Only

If only the days
stayed a little later.
If twilight held her colors
for a few extra turns on the clock,
I would've spent them loving you.

If only the seasons
lasted a little longer.
If the warm summer nights
seeped further into autumn,
I would've spent them loving you.

But something is always ending,
leaving, saying goodbye,
and I blame time,
but maybe, in truth,
it was always you.

All I know is that
I didn't get long enough
to love you.

Every Time I Close My Eyes

You can find me
where today meets tomorrow,
hidden by a night sky
that will always hold my dreams.
Isn't it beautiful,
the way you come back to me
every time I close my eyes?

My Biggest Fear

One day
I will be nothing
but a memory to you,
and you will still be
everything to me.

Playing with Matches

You were playing with matches,
and I was only too willing to burn,
just to be part of your game.

Ruinous

Since we met,
I have used every breath
in these lungs
to either love you
or miss you.

It sounds romantic,
but I think it's just ruinous.

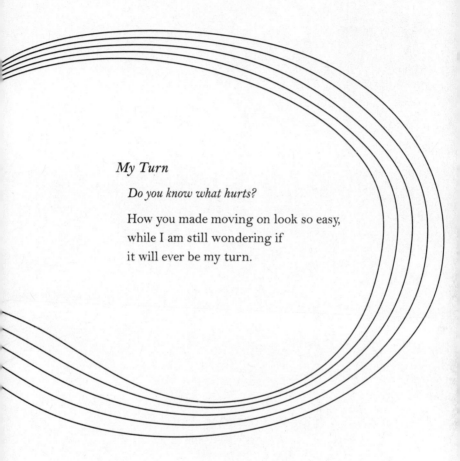

My Turn

Do you know what hurts?

How you made moving on look so easy,
while I am still wondering if
it will ever be my turn.

Regret

You weren't even mine,
but it broke my heart to lose you,
and now I live in a world
without hearing your name,
without seeing your smile,
and filled with the regret
of knowing that all the words
I felt too afraid to speak
were the ones that really mattered.

Almost

> If there's one thing
> I learned from us,
> it's that nothing aches
> quite like *almost*.

Nostalgia

Nostalgia doesn't want me to move on.
It wants me to live in the past forever
because that's where you are.

But nostalgia distorts the memories
and paints them rose-tinted.
It skips over the bad ones,
so that I almost forget there were any.

And it tries to convince me
that I still miss you, but I think
I mostly just miss feeling loved.

In Another Lifetime

In another lifetime
we watch the sun set together
at the end of every day,
and it's the only goodbye we know.

Because in another lifetime,
I like to think we made it.

More or Less

I used to wish
you had loved me
more.

But now I just wish
I had loved you
less.

Once Upon a Time

We were exactly what each other needed, once upon a time. You were looking for somewhere to rest and I wanted someone to hold.

But over time, we both changed. I barely recognized you anymore, and you never really knew me at all.

We grew apart instead of together, and the space between us became greater than the distance I could reach.

But this meant that letting go wouldn't hurt, because I had already stopped holding on.

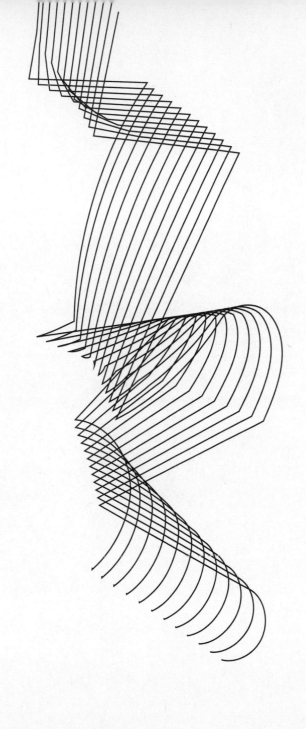

Crashing

How to Let Go

I have eyes that miss
what they've never seen
and dreams that hold me back
time and time again.

I live inside the darkness
because the rising sun
looks too much like change.

I have a bruise-colored heart
that still beats for every yesterday it has ever known,
and hands that keep reaching
for what they shouldn't.

Yet I want to let go as gracefully as the moon
when dawn greets the horizon.

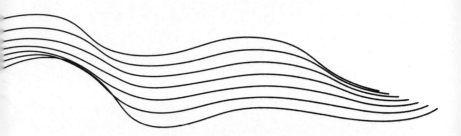

Keepsake

I'm a museum for memories.
A burial ground for broken dreams.
A hiding place for hope.

Which is to say,

I'm just a collection
of all the things I've lost.

Before the Sun Rises

I float through the days like a ghost,
drifting in and out of daydreams and nightmares.

But dusk no longer brings rest,
and dawn no longer brings newness.

And they tell me to look to the future,
but change is nowhere to be seen on the horizon,

and tomorrow has already waned
before the sun even rises.

*Things That Will Only Ever Love
from a Distance*

Parallel lines.
Two ships in the night.
The sun and the moon.
Me and you.

The Darker Season

Every part of me
falls away like the leaves,
until I am just a forest
at the end of autumn,
my colors drained,
my palms empty.
The darker season
is full of small deaths,
full of things that leave
and never come back.

The Weight of Wanting

The weight of wanting will crack ribs.
Will leave lungs gasping for air.
Will crush any fragment of happiness
it can find until sorrow blooms
in all the places joy abandoned.

The Wrong Side of Healing

Everyone tells me
that life is full of color,
but it's not always easy to see
from here. Because I'm on
the wrong side of healing
and everything just looks gray.

Some Kind of Softness

I am all
cracked bone
and splinters,
just hoping
there is some kind
of softness
waiting for me.

I fear
there are parts of me
that will never know
how to heal.

Handfuls of Regret

Every time
I reach into the past,
I come back with
handfuls of regret,
but I can't help but feel glad
to have something to hold.

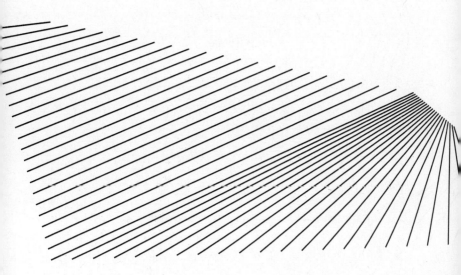

The Other Side

I am always chasing life
but never keeping up,
as if I'm following train tracks
through blurred landscapes,
but the view always changes
before my eyes can focus.

And I keep staring
through fingerprinted glass,
watching the world pass by
from behind these windows
and wondering if I will ever
find myself on the other side.

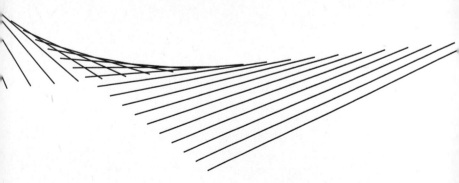

Where Have You Gone?

I miss the girl
with a sunshine smile
and sweet, innocent laughter
that had not yet been silenced.

I miss the girl
who believed in fairy tales,
and happy endings,
and that dreams could come true.

When I look in the mirror now,
there's a stranger staring at me.

I don't think that girl
is ever coming back.

Love Lived Here First

This used to be a home,
but now it's just an abandoned house
shrouded in shadows
and covered in crawling ivy.

But there was a time when
every room glowed with warmth,
because love lived here first,
long before grief.

That feels like a different lifetime,
but I open a window,
and somewhere in the distance
a bird begins to sing.

Maze

I go back down the same path
or arrive at another dead end.
I try to scramble through hedges
that leave me scratched and battered,
and I dig tunnels that never reach
the light.

Because anxiety is a maze,
and I have convinced myself
there's no way out.

Gardener

Grief is a persistent weed.

It grows in spite of the
happiness you plant.
It grows even when you try to dig it out
because its roots are always deeper than you think.
It can so easily blossom into
an entire garden of sadness.

And we are all just untrained gardeners
trying to overcome it.

Through the Devastation

I am splitting at the seams
and crumbling into the chaos.
And I fear that what breaks
can be rebuilt
only if I can find myself
in the devastation.

Reckless

I have always
been reckless with my heart,
forgiving too easily
and giving out more chances
than I should.

I fall for lies
and always believe promises,
and I say *It's okay*
when it's far from it,
just so they don't feel bad.

The worst part of all
is that I still wonder why
I keep getting hurt.

Inside My Own Mind

I have a head that's overflowing
with impossible dreams
and a heart that won't stop
aching for them.

I spend so much time
inside my own mind,
I fear I've forgotten
how it feels to live.

Murmuration

My mind is a murmuration,
a chaotic whirl of wings,
thoughts darting in and out
like starlings circling each other.

I long for stillness,
to let my feathers rest,
to escape the endless cycle
of fight or flight,

but I'm trapped
in the middle of the flock,
and I'm only just
avoiding collision.

Crumbling

We try to make
permanent homes
out of temporary people
and wonder why
the walls keep
crumbling down.

Every Time It Rained

Pain did not toughen her up
like they said it would.
She couldn't help but stay
as delicate as a wildflower,
even though she almost drowned
every time it rained.

All at Once

I am
overflowing
and
hollow
all at once,
but emptiness
is one of the
heaviest things
I have ever
had to carry.

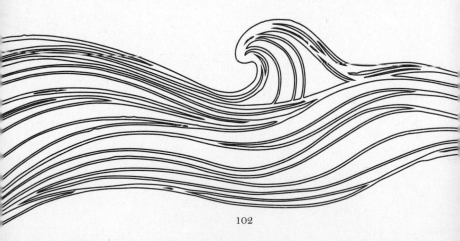

High Tide

This anxiety
is always
at high tide.

There is always
enough water
to drown.

Some Things Don't Deserve to Grow

I overwatered everything
because I wanted a garden.

In the end,
I created a flood.

Needle and Thread

I carry a needle and thread wherever I go.
I'm stuck in a constant loop
of unraveling at the smallest things
and trying to stitch myself back up
before anyone notices.

The Past

The past
follows me everywhere
like a shadow.

It whispers in my ear,
reminding me of every way
I've ever been hurt.

It pulls me back
when I try to take
a step forward.

And just like it wants, every time
I turn around to tell it to leave me alone,
I lose sight of the future.

All I Can Do

What a heartbreaking
realization it is,
that no amount of reaching
will ever be enough,
that all I can do is pray
that eventually,
the longing will turn
into something gentler,
into something
that allows me
to breathe.

A New Gravity

I live with my head in the clouds,
but now there's a new gravity
that keeps my feet on the ground,

and I just want to remember how to fly.

What It Cost Me

I'd been setting myself on fire
to be the light others needed.

It left my skin covered in burns
and my lungs full of smoke.

But I didn't know how to stop giving,
no matter what it cost me.

The Storm Inside

A dusty moonlight
filters through the trees,
but her ghost
stays hidden
in the shadows.

The storm inside her
lies silent for now;
it still swirls
in her haunted eyes.

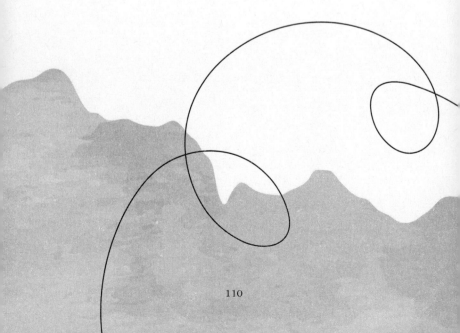

Lost

I trip over my own feet,
and when I take a step forward,
I take another two back.

I spin around in circles until I'm dizzy,
and I am the biggest obstacle
in my way.

It feels like
I'll just be lost forever.

Discarded

I am the leaves that drift
to the damp forest floor
when the wind howls
and the trees shake.
I lie discarded and hidden
at the bottom of the pile.

All around me,
the colors are fading
and I fear that I am, too.

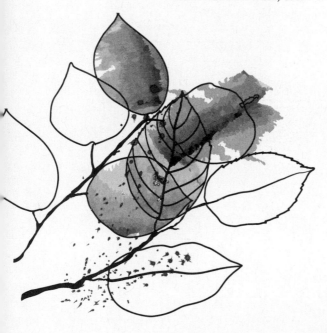

When the Sky Fell

Once upon a time,
she had the world
at her fingertips,
until suddenly, it shattered.
Now stars lie at her feet
from when the sky fell,
and she will always
be left wondering
what the universe
could've given her.

A Million Moments

I weep
for all the places of my past
I no longer recognize.

The homes that are now just houses.
The friends who are now just faces.
The lovers who are now just lessons.

Because the past
is constantly growing,
taking so much with it.

I am homesick
for a million moments
I can never return to.

Second Chances

I bruise and the marks don't ever heal, like little thunderclouds that live in my heart and rain on me from time to time.

I have never known how to stop caring, but it's not my weakness. It's my beauty. Because it's okay if moving on doesn't feel right, and forgiveness is easier than expected.

Letting go isn't always the answer, and cutting ties isn't always needed. Sometimes things just need untangling.

Some people deserve second chances (but not third and fourth and fifth), and the way you hold on to someone might just save them.

Sinkhole

The world beneath me
cracks open like a sinkhole,
and I fall back into the darkness
I had only just climbed out of.

I sit among the debris
and wonder how long it will be
until I'm strong enough
to do this again.

I wonder how many times
I will have to do this again.

Because I'm afraid
that a pattern is forming.
I'm afraid that I will never stop

falling

back

down.

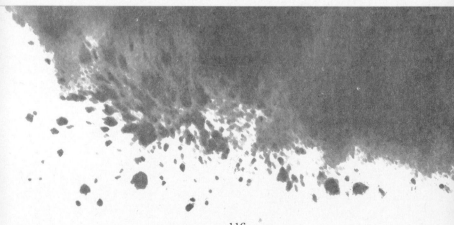

Miracle

I reach for change and hope it will notice how much I need it to find me, even if it only looks briefly in my direction.

I will show it my dreams because they are always so full of color, even when the world feels black and white. If I'm lucky, it will assure me that there's an entire kaleidoscope of shades I've never seen before, just waiting for the right moment to meet my eyes.

Maybe I've just been looking for a miracle that may never come, but there will always be a part of me that keeps holding on to hope.

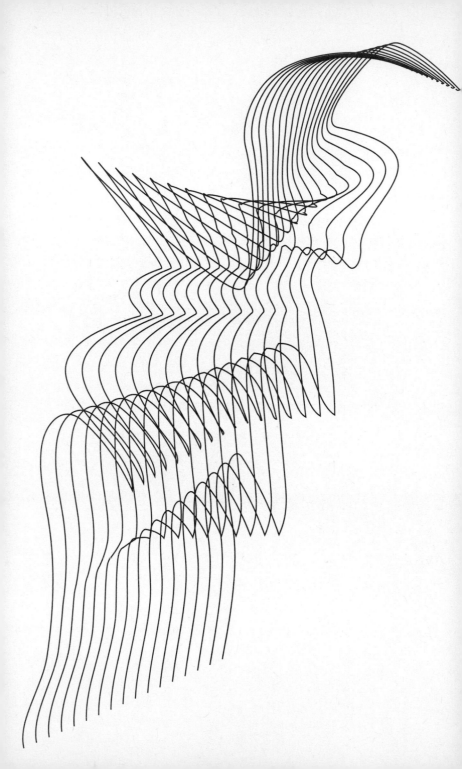

Flying

While It Lasted

I still smile when I think about you
because the memories will always be special,
even long after they've stopped being moments.

But I no longer cry myself to sleep,
and I don't even notice how empty
the bed feels when I wake up without you.

It was great while it lasted,
but sometimes good things come to an end.
And it finally feels okay that they did.

Each Day

I want to greet each day
with a smile and a brave face,
as if to tell it:

I can handle whatever you throw at me.

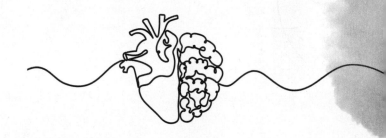

When I Feel Lonely

When I feel lonely,
I try to think of it
as quality time with my own heart,
allowing it to rest and heal.
I try to think of it
as getting to know myself better,
learning to love the parts of me
I've ignored for too long.
And I try to think of it
as finally having the clarity
to see what truly matters,
because at least I know
I will always have myself.

Hero

I will stop looking
for a happy ending
in somebody else
and write my own
fresh new beginning.

I will be the hero of my own story.
I never needed anybody else to save me.

All They Taught You

None of it was a waste.

Even if all they taught you
was what love *shouldn't* be.

A Reminder

You cannot hope to heal
when you are stuck
somewhere between
needing to get over them
and still wishing
they would come back.

Put Out the Fire

Distance is conquerable,
but I should not always be
the one left to close it.

If they burn a bridge
without even trying to cross it,
I should not be the one left
to put out the fire.

Dig Deep

It has to hurt before it can heal,
but the hardest times show us
what we're made of.

Because when you dig deep,
you will find a strength within
that you never knew you had.

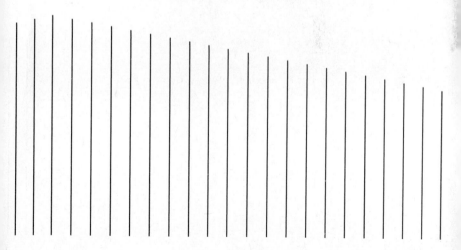

A Reason

It hurt so much to fall apart.

But I began the grueling task
of putting myself back together,
and found a reason
for shattering like this.

There were some pieces
I needed to leave behind.

Where You Belong

It's time
to leave you in the past
where you belong.
Joy existed long before
I ever met you.

It will exist again
even now that you're gone.

I Keep Going

I uproot
the mountains
I cannot climb
and walk through the fires
I cannot put out,
and no matter how much it hurts,
I keep going.

I won't let anything stand in my way.

The Only Way

I had no choice but to let go
once it started to hurt
more often than it didn't.
I couldn't keep you
if it meant losing my happiness.

In the end, sacrificing us
was the only way
to save myself.

Mixed Signals

You left it too late and wondered why I had already moved on, but false hope was taking up too much space in my heart. I needed to make room for healing.

You asked me to wait (always just a little bit longer). But I knew that mixed signals would never turn into green lights, and I wasn't made to stay in one place.

A Promise to Myself

Once I finally found peace,
I swore I'd never let anyone
ruin it again.

In the Middle

So much was lost
when I stopped reaching
more than halfway,
but everyone who
was worth keeping
met me somewhere
in the middle.

For a Little While

It might not happen for a little while,
but there will be a tomorrow
when you wake up and don't miss them.
You'll be halfway through your day
before you even think about them,
and even then you'll push the memory
to the back of your mind and carry on.

It might not happen for a little while,
but eventually you'll be able to listen to
those songs again without being reminded of them,
and you'll stop searching for their face in every crowd.
You'll throw out that sweatshirt of theirs
you'd secretly kept, and you'll discover
that your smile never depended on them at all.

It might not happen for a little while,
but healing *will* find you, and slowly fill
all the empty spaces they left behind.

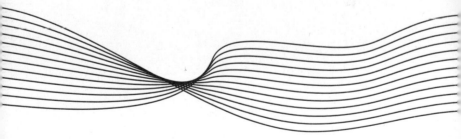

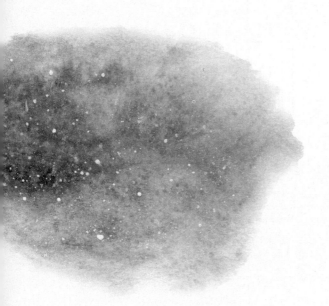

How Much?

How much of the past
are you still allowing to haunt you?

And how much of the future
are you willing to let it ruin?

Letting Go of You

It takes every ounce
of energy I have,
but I finally step
out of your grasp
and into the fresh air.

It dries the tears on my face
and awakens my soul,
and I know my heart
is too wild to ever go back
to your cages.

Because once I learn how to,
I cannot resist letting go of you.

When You Left

When you left
it felt as though I was trapped
in an everlasting winter,
but oh, how I am blooming now,
in your absence.

Present

I spend too much time inside my own mind, thinking about different days and forgetting to be present. But I think I'll slow down, live in the moment, and spend more time with reality than with dreams.

The past has gone, and no amount of overthinking can change it. The future is coming, and no amount of worrying can shape it. The present is all we have, and I want to show up for it.

I don't want to be so lost in yesterday or tomorrow that I end up missing today.

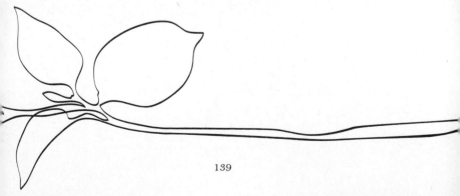

Don't Forget

Show yourself
kindness, love, and forgiveness.

Even on your worst days.
Even when you make mistakes.
Even when you think you don't deserve it.

(That's when you need it most.)

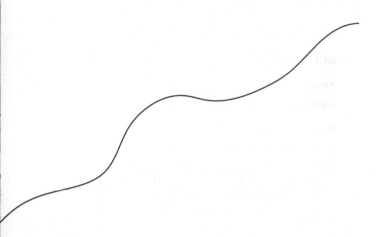

Blessing in Disguise

One day, you'll be too busy focusing on yourself to even remember them, and you'll stop wishing for them to come back, because you've seen how much brighter the future looks now.

One day, you'll smile instead of cry when someone asks about them. You'll say you hope they're happy and mean it, because you've found that healing comes from peace and not revenge.

Because one day, the pain will leave, and the reminders will become gentler, and you'll realize that sometimes, an ending can be a blessing in disguise.

For Me

I forgive you,
but *for me.*

Let Them Go

I used to think
there was nothing worse
than losing somebody,
but now I know
the worst thing
is losing yourself while
trying to hold on
to someone who
isn't meant to be
a part of your story.

The Whole World

Stop trying to build a future
out of the tiny pieces they give you.

You deserve the whole world.

The Women I Know

All the women I know
are as soft as the petal
and as sweet as the nectar,
as strong as the root,
and as sharp as the thorn.

All the women I know
are as bright as the sunshine,
and as refreshing as the rain,
as intense as the thunder,
and as powerful as the lightning.

All the women I know
are all parts flower
and all parts storm.

Grow Again

Yesterday,
I was
the wildfire.

Today,
I am
the ashes.

Tomorrow,
I will
grow again.

If You Could See

If you could see
what we have buried,
you would never
question our strength.
We have turned
pain into power
and hurt into hope.
So when you look
at our graveyards,
you see only gardens.

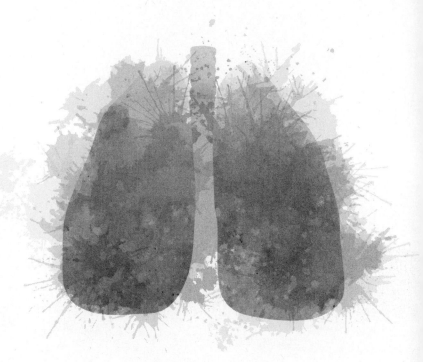

A Setting Free of the Lungs

Letting go
is a setting free
of the lungs.
An exhale.

Because You Are

Buy yourself the flowers.
Hold your own hand.
Treat yourself to dinner.
Enjoy your own company.
Remind yourself that you're
beautiful and worthy and powerful,
because you are,
and you don't need a man
to tell you.

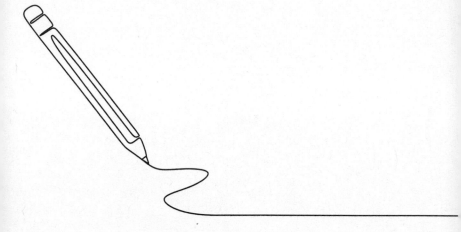

A Letter to My Younger Self

Life tried to break us but we didn't let it. When we felt broken, we never were. We left those pieces behind because they no longer fit right.

The heartbreak didn't last forever, even when it felt like it would. True love found us and it was worth the wait.

Every time we felt like the world was ending, a new season began. And these days, there is honesty in your smile and happiness in your heart. So, hold on a little longer, because I promise—*those days are just around the corner.*

No Matter

I bloom more than I break,
and flourish more than I fall apart.
No matter how many times I lose my way,
I know that hope will always find me again.

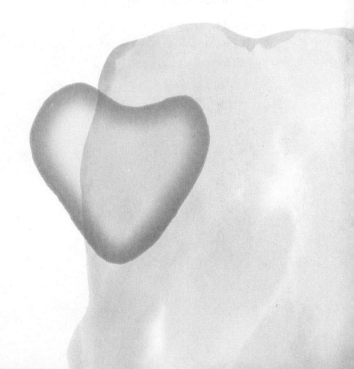

Strength

When did you discover your strength?

When they didn't apologize
and I still learned to forgive.

When they didn't apologize
and I still learned to heal.

Greener

The grass always seems
greener somewhere,
but do not weep when you see
how their flowers are blooming.

Just because yours
are taking longer to grow,
doesn't mean your garden
won't be beautiful.

Soft

Don't mistake
this tenderness
for weakness.

It has taken
incredible strength
to remain this soft,

despite the wars
and weapons
and wounds.

When You Need To

When you need to,
close the curtains.
Bury yourself under the blankets.
Cry until your eyes sting
and your head aches.
Let it all out
and then,
start again.
Take a deep breath.
Dry your eyes.
Open the windows.
Because it's okay
to hide from the world
on the days it does not feel kind,
as long as you always come back.

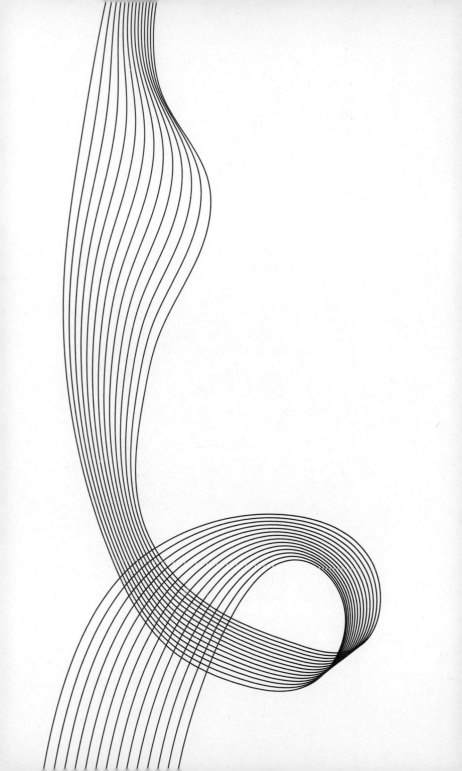

Landing

My Light

They told me I'm a storm,
but I'm the entire sky.

My heart is laced with indigo
and I weep until the rivers overflow.
I become the thunder and lightning
because I need to be felt.

But these dark days are okay.
These dark days do not define me.

My light will always find a way
to burst through any clouds.

Exactly on Time

I used to wish
we had found each other sooner.

But fate was on our side,
and we were exactly on time.

Shifting

Do you feel it?
Something in the air
is shifting,
only softly,
but still,
enough to know
that the season
is finally changing,
that I am becoming
vibrant again.

Some Stories

We were reading our story
and my eyes skipped ahead.
I expected the word *goodbye*
to glare back at me, but
we turned each page to find
something even better on the next one.

Pages turned into chapters,
yet still, neither of us ever
wanted to close the book.
Some stories don't have to end.
Some stories are made to last forever.

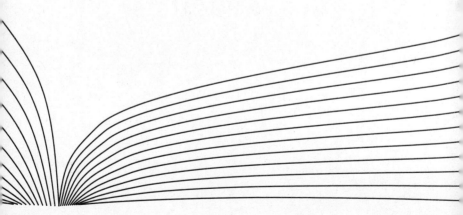

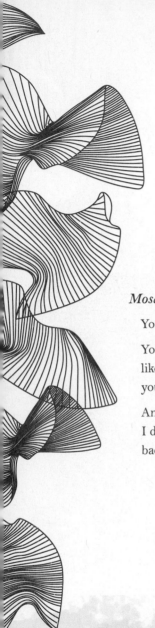

Mosaic

You didn't try to fix me.

You loved all my broken fragments
like I was the most incredible mosaic
you had ever seen.

And you held my hand while
I discovered how to piece myself
back together.

The Visitor

When the hurt arrives
on my doorstep,
I let it in.

I used to lock all the doors
and draw the curtains,
but heartbreak
will still come knocking,
no matter how high you build your walls.

So now I make it tea,
play its favorite sad songs on repeat,
and while it's wallowing,
I prepare for happiness to come back:
tidy away the clutter of memories,
turn the porch light on,
plant seeds of hope in the front garden.

And then I wait.
Because the pain is just a visitor.
I know it isn't here to stay.

All the Glorious Days

When today
feels full of ache,
I remember
all the glorious days
that have been.
I remember
all the glorious days
that are yet to come.

What Matters

This is the kind of love
you see in movies
and read about in books,
the kind you want to
shout from the rooftops until
the whole world stops to listen.

This is the kind of love
that finds you when you're lost
and shows you what home feels like,
the kind that reminds you
how it feels to love
without the need for walls.

It isn't always perfect
(because nothing ever is),
but we never give up trying.

Out of Windows

No matter
how many doors close,
I never stop looking
out of windows.

With Her Light

Healing hangs over me like a thundercloud most of the time. Her rain falls fiercely, like the sky is crying for me, and her thunder sounds like a heart breaking in two.

She is a storm that can feel like she's taking forever to pass, but the sun comes back and reminds me how to keep growing with her light.

The Greatest Gift

The universe
hasn't always been
on my side,
but to know you
and love you
and be loved by you
is the greatest gift
it ever could've given me.

Atlas

Every day leaves its mark.
Some like laughter lines,
others like scars.
But each and every one
comes together to create
an atlas that shows
the story of our lives—
everywhere we've ever been
and everyone we've ever loved.

If I Stumble

Putting one foot
in front of the other
feels like the hardest thing
I could ever have to do.
But you hold my hand
to remind me you'll be there
to catch me if I stumble,
and it suddenly feels
a little easier.

The Importance of Rain

The earth cracks open
and I learn
the importance
of rain.

Everything needs
softness in order to grow.

Home

Healing is a new house
and acceptance is the key,
and today I am finally moving in.

I have walked miles to get here,
through fields of forgiveness
and down roads of recovery,

and this time, I won't need to hide pain
in the attic, because I no longer
feel the need to bring it with me.

I arrive to see that the doormat reads *Welcome*
and the walls inside are brightly painted,
and when I unpack joy, it fills the room.

And it feels good to start again.
It feels good to finally
be home.

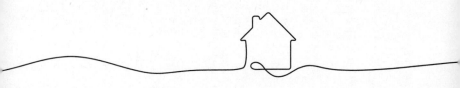

Smile

It's okay
if your smile is lost.
At least you're being honest
about how you feel.
But never give up
searching for it,
because hope is buried
somewhere below.
Just dig through the layers of
heartbreak
to find it again.

Plot Twist

I found you
when I least expected it,
like a plot twist
I never saw coming,
and you ended up being
the greatest part of my story.

All Four of the Seasons

I have always
been afraid of change.
But there is something beautiful
in all four of the seasons,
and I know the sun will keep
coming back for me.

As Long as We've Got Each Other

We've never needed much to be happy—
even the simplest times are still special.
Like Sunday afternoons and raindrops on windows,
grocery shopping and winding country roads,
worn pajamas and cozy blankets,
and our favorite film for the fifth time.
Because we've never needed much to be happy.
Every day is perfect as long as we've got each other.

A Way Through

Lately I've noticed
that joy is slowly
weaving its way back in,
like the sun finding
even the darkest corners
just to remind us
that the light will always
find a way through.

How to Fly

I will mend
these broken wings
and teach myself
how to fly again,
because my dreams
are nearer than I thought,
and I don't need
to close my eyes
to keep them in sight.

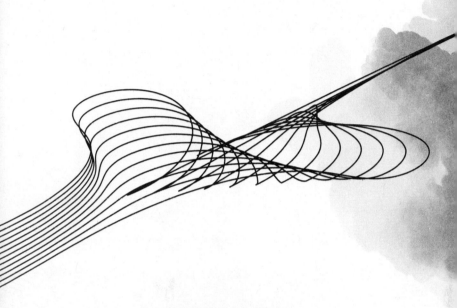

The Best Things Take Time

It's okay
if you're healing slowly.

Have you seen how
the oak tree grows?
Have you felt how
the seasons change?

The Way You're Growing

There are better days ahead.
Days with no tears and smiles that belong.
Days filled with the sound of so much joy
that sorrow is barely a whisper.
Because scars heal and bruises fade,
and the ache is just a sign
of the way you're growing.

All I Ever Wanted

All I ever wanted
was someone who would
love me both softly and fiercely,
feel like home and an adventure,
and keep me feeling young
as we grow old together.

And—god, you are exactly
what I wished for.

A New Dawn

Sunrise is the most beautiful reminder
that starting again is always okay,
no matter how many times you have to do it.

Everything I Could Ever Need

You're my shelter
when I'm all raging storm,
and my atlas when I'm lost.

You're my rock
when I'm all crashing waves,
and my white flag when I'm a war.

And you are everything
I could ever need
and more.

Breath by Breath

If taking it day by day
feels overwhelming,
you can take it step by step.
And if you stumble,
you can take it breath by breath.

By My Side

You've stayed by my side
through all my seasons,

and no matter how cold it gets,
you always feel like summer.

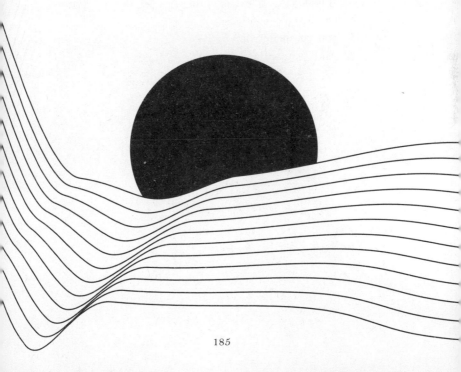

In Bloom

I am blooming like a flower.
My petals are bolder than ever
and my roots are becoming
stronger all the time,
and I keep growing,
with the rays and with the rain.

The Journey to Love

The journey to love
is often long and lonely.
There are obstacles and dead ends.
There is heartbreak at every corner.
But then we cross paths,
and suddenly, everything aligns.
The road ahead is clear,
and the pain of the past
has reason and purpose.

All of it was leading me to you.

Around the Corner

I am no longer
afraid of the dark.
There are flowers
that still bloom,
and birds that still sing,
and I know that there is
always another dawn waiting
around the corner.

Little Moments

I don't want much—
just time.

I want to live
in the little moments with you

and to witness them
add up to a lifetime.

Healing

It won't happen overnight,
but one day you'll notice
that your smile is a little wider,
that it shines a little brighter in your eyes,
that your laugh is a little louder,
that you feel it a little deeper in your soul,
that your heart feels a little lighter,
that you can breathe easier again.
Because even though you thought
it would never be possible,
one day you'll notice
that you're healing.

Moving Forward

I get back up every time I trip,
and maybe that's all that really matters.
That I keep finding my feet.
That I keep moving forward.

You and Me

> I just hope
> it's you and me
> until the end.